T0147368

Keys to Becoming

A Virtuous Woman

Devotional and Journal

Keys to Becoming

A Virtuous Woman

Devotional and Journal

Dr. Latrina W. Jenkins

iUniverse, Inc.
New York   Bloomington

Keys to Becoming A Virtuous Woman

Devotional and Journal

iUniverse books may be ordered through booksellers or by contacting:

iUniverse
1663 Liberty Drive
Bloomington, IN 47403
www.iuniverse.com
1-800-Authors (1-800-288-4677)

ISBN: 978-1-4401-0572-2 (pbk)
ISBN: 978-1-4401-0573-9 (ebk)

Printed in the United States of America

All scriptures are taken from the King James Version of the Bible.

iUniverse rev. date: 12/29/2008

Dedication

I would like to dedicate this devotional and journal to my natural and spiritual mother, Mother Loretta Ward; and to all the women of New Life. You have encouraged me in more ways than you can imagine. I release showers of blessings and love into your life.

Contents

Introduction

What is a "devotional?" Why is it important to have a devotional guide? **A devotional is *a short religious service. It may also be defined as an exercise that relates to worship.*** A devotional will assist you in developing a closer bond and relationship with God. It usually consists of day by day chapters and daily prayers you may read.

In the society in which we live, many women are clueless concerning their role as a household manager. Though many were raised in the care of mothers, grandmothers and other female caretakers, they were never educated on the biblically correct approach to womanhood. The book of **Proverbs (Chapter 31)** is a very powerful guide and may be very instrumental in equipping women of God. It gives us empowering guidelines on how to become that "virtuous woman" God intended for us to be. He intended for us to be holy and righteous women; brilliant and devoted wives and mothers. The virtuous woman is one who trains and teaches her children using the highest morals, the spirit of excellence, and is filled with Godly wisdom. Her husband will be grateful for such an anointed vessel for she is honorable and is highly worthy of praise. We should all strive to be the *"Proverbs 31 virtuous woman".*

It is time to move forward in Jesus, our Lord and Savior so that we may experience the abundance of life that He has designed for us as virtuous women. We, as women of God must recognize that we are more precious and valuable than rubies. We are priceless! This devotional guide will help to develop you into that woman of virtue that you desire to be. Keep in mind: *"many daughters have done virtuously, but thou excellest them all". (Proverbs 31:29).*

These twenty-five keys will motivate you, and will also provide you with with the confidence required to overcome the daily struggles you encounter as you strive to become all that God has intended for you to be; *"A Virtuous Woman"!* My daughters God is calling for virtuousness! Believe it, walk in it, live it, it belongs to you!

"Who can find a virtuous woman? For her price is far above Rubies".

Proverbs 31:10

A Woman of Holiness

"But as he which hath called you is holy, so be ye holy in all manner of conversation; Because it is written, Be ye holy; for I am holy." (I Peter 1:15-16)

It is of uttermost importance to live a life that is pleasing to God. We should not long to please our flesh or our selfish desires, but instead, we should seek to fulfill the desires of the Almighty God. When we as virtuous women take a stand to live in a manner that is consistent with the divine will of God, we will live a holy lifestyle.

Virtuous Prayer:

Oh Heavenly Father, help me to live a holy life; one that is pleasing, to you; one that satisfies the desires you have for my life.

A Woman of Trust

"In God have I put my trust: I will not be afraid what man can do unto me" (Psalms 56:11).

Knowing that we can trust God makes us feel good about our relationship with Him. It denounces outside forces and unhealthy influences. We, as women of God, must be taught how to trust God totally. Quite often we put our trust in man, herbs, and medicine. Believe in the power of God He will come through for you! God is exceptionally trust worthy. If there was ever a time to put all your trust in Him, the time is now!

Virtuous Prayer: Oh Lord, help me to believe in you with all my heart not just part of it, teach me to trust in you persistently.

A Woman of Joy

"Then he said unto them, Go your way, eat the fat, and drink the sweet, and send portions unto them for whom nothing is prepared: for this day is holy unto our Lord: neither be ye sorry; for the joy of the Lord is your strength" (*Nehemiah 8:10*).

Be joyful in everything you do. Joy is our source of strength. No one desires to be around sorrow it brings the spirit man down. Learn how to smile, laugh, and be cheerful. The Lord is our life and His joy is our foundation of strength.

Virtuous Prayer: Father God, help me to keep a smile and not a frown. Keep me full of the medicine of laughter.

A Woman of Security

"She is not afraid of the snow for her household: for all her household are clothed with scarlet". (Proverbs 31:21).

Our ark of safety is in our Lord Jesus Christ. It is only through Him that our inner fight against transgression can be completely dominated. It is only through the precious blood of Jesus that we can break away from the snares of the enemy and receive freedom in all areas of our life.

Virtuous Prayer: Heavenly Father, keep me safe and secure in your arms and I know I will not be moved. I denounce all fear out of my life and release all insecurities. Amen.

A Woman of Strength and Power

"The LORD is my light and my salvation; whom shall I fear? The LORD is the strength of my life; of whom shall I be afraid?" (Psalm27: 1)

We must learn to triumph over all the uncertainties in our lives. The Lord is our light in every gloomy situation; he will give us supernatural strength. Use your God given strength and authority and you will always see the light of your salvation.

Virtuous Prayer: Father God, assist me in denouncing all manner of fear from my life completely. I pray for strength and power in this very hour that I speak. Thank you Lord.

A Woman of Purity

"Who shall ascend into the hill of the LORD? Or who shall stand in his holy place? He that hath clean hands, and a pure heart; who hath not lifted up his soul unto vanity, nor sworn deceitfully. He shall receive the blessing from the LORD, and righteousness from the God of his salvation." (Psalm 24:3-5)

We should understand the certainty of the covenant relationship that God desires to have with us: As *virtuous women,* we must put away every part of evil and malice so that we may dwell in the standards set by God for the chosen remnant that serves Him with clean hands, pure hearts, and righteous living.

Virtuous Prayer: Oh Father, give me a clean and pure heart and wash my hands from all unrighteousness so that I may receive all the blessings you have in store for me.

A Woman of Righteousness

"A man shall not be established by wickedness: but the root of the righteous shall not be moved. A virtuous woman is a crown to her husband: but she that maketh ashamed is as rottenness in his bones. The thoughts of the righteous are right: but the counsels of the wicked are deceit."

(Proverbs 12:3-5)

The Lord desires for us to live upright and Godly before Him. When you are rooted and grounded in the things of God, you cannot be moved because of the strong foundation that rests assured. The righteous are well established and the wicked shall never be secure.

Virtuous Prayer: Heavenly Father, keep me upright before you so that I may stand firm. Keep me with righteous and virtuous thoughts.

A Woman of Clean Vessels

"But the man that shall be unclean, and shall not purify himself, that soul shall be cut off from among the congregation, because he hath defiled the sanctuary of the LORD: the water of separation hath not been sprinkled upon him; he is unclean. And it shall be a perpetual statute unto them, that he that sprinkleth the water of separation shall wash his clothes; and he that toucheth the water of separation shall be unclean until even. And whatsoever the unclean person toucheth shall be unclean; and the soul that toucheth it shall be unclean until even."

(Numbers 19:20-22)

A virtuous woman is one who is clean within, as well as on the outside. Keep your self pure, stay away from all filthiness and uncleanness which may pollute your sprit.

Virtuous Prayer: Dear Father, thank you for keeping me free from spots and wrinkles and allowing me to stay clean before your presence.

A Woman with Vessels of Honor

"For this is the will of God, even your sanctification, that ye should abstain from fornication: That every one of you should know how to possess his vessel in sanctification and honor; Not in the lust of concupiscence, even as the Gentiles which know not God":

(I. Thessalonians 4:3-5)

It is indeed an honor and privilege to stand before our King in true sanctification. Don't allow the adversary to contaminate the vessel you have worked so hard to become.

Virtuous Prayer: Father, help me stand firm and keep me with vessels of honor. Lord thank you for allowing me to walk in honor and integrity.

A Woman of Faith

"Thou gavest me no kiss: but this woman, since the time I came in, hath not ceased to kiss my feet. My head with oil thou didst not anoint: but this woman hath anointed my feet with ointment. Wherefore I say unto thee, Her sins, which are many, are forgiven; for she loved much: but to whom little is forgiven, the same loveth little. And he said unto her, Thy sins are forgiven. And they that sat at meat with him began to say within themselves, Who is this that forgiveth sins also? And he said to the woman, Thy faith hath saved thee; go in peace".

(St. Luke 7: 45-50)

Without faith it is impossible to please God. He yearns for us to trust and believe in His spoken word. Our soul should seek to please Him. We should be assured by faith knowing that He will come through for us.

Virtuous Prayer: Heavenly Father, I thank you for increasing my faith and allowing me never to doubt your unfailing word.

A Woman of Purpose

"Now when Jesus was in Bethany, in the house of Simon the leper, There came unto him a woman having an alabaster box of very precious ointment, and poured it on his head, as he sat at meat. But when his disciples saw it, they had indignation, saying, To what purpose is this waste? For this ointment might have been sold for much, and given to the poor. When Jesus understood it, he said unto them, Why trouble ye the woman? for she hath wrought a good work upon me".

(St. Matthew 26:6-10)

Women of God, you have most definitely been called according to His purpose! We must continually strive for bigger and better goals in life. Some of the things you do may seem unusual, but consider what you are doing as a good work. You were created with a purpose in mind, the things you do should be in line with that purpose. Remember, you are a woman of virtue.

Virtuous Prayer: Father, I thank you for allowing me to walk in and understand my God given purpose. Thank you for not allowing my assignments to go to waste.

A Woman of Destiny

"When the Lord shall have washed away the filth of the daughters of Zion, and shall have purged the blood of Jerusalem from the midst thereof by the spirit of judgment, and by the spirit of burning. And the LORD will create upon every dwelling place of mount Zion, and upon her assemblies, a cloud and smoke by day, and the shining of a flaming fire by night: for upon all the glory shall be a defense. And there shall be a tabernacle for a shadow in the daytime from the heat, and for a place of refuge, and for a covert from storm and from rain".

(Isaiah 4:4-6)

There is a great destiny ahead of you, and your latter shall be greater than your past. The Lord has put a shield of protection around you, daughter of Zion. He has given you a safe haven. Begin to speak a farewell to unfulfilled and disappointed dreams. You are a woman who is destined for greatness. Grab hold to a new level of self-assurance and live a life of purpose. Walk in victory!

Virtuous Prayer: Father God, I thank you for opening my understanding and allowing me to recognize that you have the perfect dwelling place for me.

A Woman of Praise

"I will extol thee, my God, O King; and I will bless thy name for ever and ever. Every day will I bless thee; and I will praise thy name for ever and ever. Great is the LORD, and greatly to be praised; and his greatness is unsearchable".

(Psalm145:1-3)

Keep a continual praise in your mouth. Praise is a weapon that will destroy the adversary every time! Continually offer up a sacrifice of praise to God. Keep your mouth and belly full of praise. Present God a praise that He will inhabit. He desires to dwell in a temple that is filled with total praise. You will experience the magnitude of God through your offering of praise.

Virtuous Prayer: Oh Lord, I will praise thy holy name with the fruit of my lips. I will rejoice in you always and be thankful and bless your marvelous name. I will send many praises unto you and I am grateful to have a true praise, I will continue to pay tribute to you through my praise.

A Woman of Worship

"Give unto the LORD, O ye mighty, give unto the LORD glory and strength. Give unto the LORD the glory due unto his name; worship the LORD in the beauty of holiness".

(Psalm 29:1-2)

Through His holy word, God has revealed His enormous and never-ending love for us. The holy temple curtain was torn in two as symbol that mankind may cross the threshold to the Holy of Holies, and have a complete, intimate connection with our Heavenly Father. We can worship Him in the true beauty of holiness.

Virtuous Prayer: Thank you Jesus, I will bow down before you and worship you for the enormous love and sacrifices you have made for me. I will forever be the woman of worship you have called me to be. Thank you for leading me daily through the spirit of worship.

A Woman of Favor

"And it was so, when the king saw Esther the queen standing in the court, that she obtained favor in his sight: and the king held out to Esther the golden sceptre that was in his hand. So Esther drew near, and touched the top of the sceptre. Then said the king unto her, What wilt thou, queen Esther? and what is thy request? it shall be even given thee to the half of the kingdom".

(Ester 5:2-3)

Women of the highest God, you are blessed and highly favored. Get ready to walk in all the blessings that God has for you as a woman of favor. Get ready for the abundance that comes with those who are favor-minded. You are God's favorite.

Virtuous Prayer: Oh Heavenly Father, I thank you for keeping me favor minded and allowing me to have faith to endure, granting me all my petitions that have come by favor.

A Woman of Health

"Beloved, I wish above all things that thou mayest prosper and be in health, even as thy soul prospereth".

(3 John 2)

When you are confronted with a circumstance that seems to be impossible, a condition in which you don't see a way of escape, know in assurance that there is a healing balm. There is a healing path for you. You are not forgotten, for the Lord knows those who are His. *(A Pathway to Divine Healings)*

Virtuous Prayer: Lord I Thank you, for when I cried unto you, you heard my cry and have healed me from all sickness and disease.

A Woman of Wealth

"*Wealth and riches shall be in his house: and his righteousness endureth for ever. Unto the upright there ariseth light in the darkness: he is gracious, and full of compassion, and righteous*".

(*Psalm112: 3-4*)

God has given you creative power to get wealth, use it! You have creativity so start by birthing something that will take you to a new dimension of wealth. You have been empowered through righteous living to walk in a wealthy place, you deserve it.

Virtuous Prayer: Father, I would like to thank you for walking me into that wealthy place. I thank you for a place of peace, love, joy and happiness. I am a woman of prosperity and wealth I praise you for it amen.

A Woman of Peace

"Therefore being justified by faith, we have peace with God through our Lord Jesus Christ: By whom also we have access by faith into this grace wherein we stand, and rejoice in hope of the glory of God".

(Romans 5: 1-2)

There is nothing like peace. We *have peace with God through our Lord Jesus Christ.* Don't allow anyone to deprive you of the peace and abundant life that God has designed for you to have. **Choose the right way, walk circumspectly before Him and you will have a peaceful life.**

Virtuous Prayer: Father God, make me a woman of peace, especially in your holy temple. I thank you, for when I saw violence, I began to proclaim peace and safety. Father, when I felt disagreement, I didn't bend, but I broadened the hand of reconciliation.

A Woman of Happiness

"Happy is he that hath the God of Jacob for his help, whose hope is in the LORD his God: which made heaven, and earth, the sea, and all that therein is: which keepeth truth for ever":

(Palm 146: 5-6)

If you have the Lord on your side, you should have happiness. Don't allow the enemy to steal your joy. Many Christians walk around with unhappiness and it causes others to wonder "should I become a Christian?"

Virtuous Prayer: Father I thank you for the happiness that dwells deeply inside me. I understand that all the joyfulness I need is inside me, because you live within me. Father release the joy that you have given me into the lives of others, and allow them to see the true happiness that comes from you.

A Woman of Love

"And now abideth faith, hope, charity, these three; but the greatest of these is charity".

(I. Corinthians 13: 13)

God sent His only begotten Son into the world. that we might live through Him. That is love! He made the ultimate sacrifice, and died that we may live. There is no greater love. To be a woman of love, you must like Jesus give an unconditional, self-sacrificing love which is called agape, love all humanity!

Virtuous Prayer: Lord I thank you for loving me when I didn't love myself. You taught me how to love. I will forever be grateful to you by showing the same love towards others.

A Woman of Deity

"Then spake Eli'sha unto the woman, whose son he had restored to life, saying, Arise, and go thou and thine household, and sojourn wheresoever thou canst sojourn: for the LORD hath called for a famine; and it shall also come upon the land seven years. And the woman arose, and did after the saying of the man of God: and she went with her household, and sojourned in the land of the Philistines seven years".

(I. Kings 8: 1-2)

Being a woman of deity and a woman held in high regard and respect is truly important. We must live according to the principles God has set for us as virtuous and holy women. No matter what has taken place in your life, embrace deity and continue to trust and obey His every command.

Virtuous Prayer: Lord, I thank you for not allowing me to lose my deity. In spite of my condition, you have been a sustainer. I thank you Jesus, for I am a woman living in deity.

A Woman of Prayer

"And when he had considered the thing, he came to the house of Mary the mother of John, whose surname was Mark; where many were gathered together praying".

(Acts 12:12)

Prayer is our communication with God. Praying gives us that personal experience that we long for; a heavenly connection with our Lord. According to His word, if we ask anything according to His will, He hears us. If we know that He hears us, we should also know that we will have whatever we asked of Him.

Virtuous Prayer: Heavenly Father, I submit my- self to you through prayer. Father I seek to please you and I will be the intercessor that you have call me to be. Father I am willing to stand in the gap, and be a woman of prayer.

A Woman of Vision

"Yea, and certain women also of our company made us astonished, which were early at the sepulchre; And when they found not his body, they came, saying, that they had also seen a vision of angels, which said that he was alive. And certain of them which were with us went to the sepulchre, and found it even so as the women had said: but him they saw not".

(Luke 24: 22-24)

A *woman of vision* is one who is complete. She is a woman with revelation as well as impartation. She is a woman that can recognize God, and is able to hear from Him. A *women of Vision* serves as a challenge to the adversary. She is definitely an eye opener. The world stands in need of more eye-openers.

Virtuous Prayer: Father God, I thank you that I am a creative thinker. I thank you for giving me the spirit to create and the ability to see things and make them happen.

A Woman of Virtue

"Finally, brethren, whatsoever things are true, whatsoever things are honest, whatsoever things are just, whatsoever things are pure, whatsoever things are lovely, whatsoever things are of good report; if there be any virtue, and if there be any praise, think on these things".

(Philippians 4: 8)

A woman of virtue is a woman that is in direct control. She is physically powerful, intelligent and has integrity. A virtuous woman is one who is unadulterated. She is upright, and she fears God. She possesses the accepted code of behavior. She is fit and does not act out of character.

Virtuous Prayer: Oh Lord, I thank you for the strength to strive to and actually become that proverbs 31 woman. I am a woman who is unadulterated, one who refrains from sexual relationships with anyone other than my husband. I thank you for being a decent, pure and holy woman of God.

A Woman of New Life

"Therefore we are buried with him by baptism into death: that like as Christ was raised up from the dead by the glory of the Father, even so we also should walk in newness of life. For if we have been planted together in the likeness of his death, we shall be also in the likeness of his resurrection":

(Romans 6:4-5)

A newness of life: This kind of transformation is only possible through the modification and grace of God. He desires for us to live in a newness of life that comes through the Holy Spirit. As we yield to the sincerity of the Spirit, new fruit develop and give birth to love, joy, peace, patience, kindness, goodness, faithfulness, gentleness and self-control (**Galatians 5:22-23**). You will then experience the fulfillment and gratification of a woman who has found "New Life".

Virtuous Prayer: Heavenly Father, thank you for the reassurance that you have given me. Father I thank you that I can come to you boldly before the throne of grace. I thank you for newness of life and deliverance. Without you, it would not have been possible. Amen.

Virtuous & Holy

I am a virtuous woman.

I am a holy woman.

I am an example of what God can do.

I am a pure woman.

I am a righteous woman.

I am a clean vessel.

I am a vessel of honor.

I am a woman of power.

I am a woman of faith.

I am a woman of purpose.

I am a woman of destiny.

I am a woman of praise.

I am a woman of worship.

I am a woman of favor.

I am a woman of health.

I am a woman of wealth.

I am a woman of peace.

I am a woman of happiness.

I am a woman of joy.

I am a woman of love.

I am a woman of deity.

I am God's chosen virtuous & holy woman.

I am a blessed and highly favored woman of God.

Author Dr. Latrina W. Jenkins

"Give her of the fruit of her hands; and let her own works praise her in the gates".

Proverbs 31:31

Virtuous Thoughts

Many women desire to have a stronger, closer relationship with God. In actuality, many women highly desire to obtain a virtuous and holy lifestyle. So much negativity has been spoken into our spirits, not to mention the hurt and pain that has devastated our intellect and well being. As women of God, we need to have appropriate directions in our life. The very next time you are feeling a bit disgusted, confused, lost or perhaps at the verge of giving up remember that there is a living hope in Jesus! Three keys that can help you get through difficult times are: *trust in God, wisdom, and listening to the voice of the Lord.*

- ✓ **Trust**
- ✓ **Wisdom**
- ✓ **The Voice of God**

Trust

"*Let not mercy and truth forsake thee: bind them about thy neck; write them upon the table of thine heart:*

So shalt thou find favour and good under-standing in the sight of God and man.

Trust in the LORD with all thine heart; and lean not unto thine own understanding.

In all thy ways acknowledge him, and he shall direct thy paths".

Proverbs 3:3-6

Wisdom

"Get wisdom, get understanding: forget it not; neither decline from the words of my mouth.

Forsake her not, and she shall preserve thee: love her, and she shall keep thee.

Wisdom is the principal thing; therefore get wisdom: and with all thy getting get understanding".

Proverbs 4:5-7

The Voice of God

"Give unto the LORD, O ye mighty, give unto the LORD glory and strength.

Give unto the LORD the glory due unto his name; worship the LORD in the beauty of holiness.

The voice of the LORD is upon the waters: the God of glory thundereth: the LORD is upon many waters.

The voice of the LORD is powerful; the voice of the LORD is full of majesty".

Psalms 29:1-4

Virtuous Thoughts

_____

_____

_____

_____

_____

_____

_____

_____

Virtuous Thoughts

Virtuous Thoughts

Virtuous Thoughts

Virtuous Thoughts

_____

_____

_____

_____

_____

_____

_____

_____

Virtuous Thoughts

_____

_____

_____

_____

_____

_____

_____

_____

Virtuous Thoughts

Virtuous Thoughts

Virtuous Thoughts

_____

_____

_____

_____

_____

_____

_____

_____

Virtuous Thoughts

Virtuous Thoughts

Virtuous Thoughts

Virtuous Thoughts

Virtuous Thoughts

Notes

Notes

Notes

Notes

Notes

Notes

Notes

Contact: Dr. Latrina Jenkins International Ministries, Inc. to purchase her authored books:

- *Keys to Becoming a Virtuous Woman Devotional and Journal*

- *Keys to Becoming a Virtuous Woman*

- *A Pathway to Divine Healings*

- *Information on conferences, speaking engagements, and other excellent products.*

Dr. Latrina Jenkins International Ministries, Inc.

P. O. Box 667215

Pompano Beach, FL 33066

Email: dljministries@yahoo.com

Website: www.dljministries.org or www.myspace.com/drlatrinajenkins

Dr. Latrina Jenkins International Ministries, Inc.

Administrative Offices

600 S. W. 3rd Street

Pompano Beach, Fl 33060